I0890341

Words of Comfort

Publications International, Ltd.

Scripture quotations from *The Holy Bible, King James Version*

Images from Shutterstock.com

Louis Weber, CEO
Publications International, Ltd.
8140 Lehigh Avenue
Morton Grove, IL 60053

ISBN: 978-1-63938-813-4

Manufactured in China.

8 7 6 5 4 3 2 1

Let's get social!
@Publications_International
@PublicationsInternational
www.pilbooks.com

TABLE OF CONTENTS

INTRODUCTION

And he said unto her, Daughter, be of good comfort: thy faith hath made thee whole; go in peace.

—Luke 8:48

Like the woman who reached out to Jesus in the hope of a cure for her long illness, we turn to the Lord in times of infirmity, grief, and distress, in hopes of receiving healing, comfort, and peace. *Words of Comfort* has prayers and Bible verses for those times when you need to bring your problems to God. The book is divided into eight chapters, each dealing with a common problem, such as fear, loss, or confusion. You can flip through the chapter to find a prayer or reflection that resonates with you, and use its words to pray or as a springboard to develop your own words.

Grace be to you and peace from God our Father, and from the Lord Jesus Christ. Blessed be God, even the Father of our Lord Jesus Christ, the Father of mercies, and the God of all comfort; Who comforteth us in all our tribulation, that we may be able to comfort them which are in any trouble, by the comfort wherewith we ourselves are comforted of God.

—2 Corinthians 1:2–4

ENCOURAGEMENT
in Times of Fear

Be strong and of a good courage, fear not, nor be afraid of them: for the Lord thy God, he it is that doth go with thee; he will not fail thee, nor forsake thee.

—Deuteronomy 31:6

Seeking courage, Lord, I bundle my fears and place them in your hands.

They're too heavy for me, too weighty even to ponder in this moment, but such shadowy terrors shrink to size in my mind and—how wonderful!—wither to nothing in your grasp.

Fear thou not; for I am with thee: be not dismayed; for I am thy God.

—Isaiah 41:10

We respond to stresses in our lives with either fear or faith. Fear is a great threat to our faith. That's why we read often in the scriptures the directive, "Fear not." The closer we draw to God, the more our fears diminish.

Lord,

I see a robin's egg hatching, and am set free from my doubts and fretting. For, while life is not always filled with joy and happiness, I know it is always held in your hand. Thank you.

Amen.

Wherefore comfort yourselves together, and edify one another, even as also ye do.

—1 Thessalonians 5:11

Although our eyes should always be turned above toward God, sometimes we can do with a reminder of God's work just a little bit closer to home. The faith of others can serve as a reminder or an inspiration to strengthen our own faith. Just as we should provide encouragement to others, we can draw on others to help steady ourselves.

God of New Life,

Enliven my imagination, so that I
can see through today's troubles
to coming newness. Surround me
with your caring so that I can live
as if the new has already begun.

Amen.

Come, thou long-expected Jesus,
Born to set thy people free;
From our fears and sin release us;
Let us find our rest in thee.
—Charles Wesley

But Joshua the son of Nun, which standeth before thee, he shall go in thither: encourage him: for he shall cause Israel to inherit it.

—Deuteronomy 1:38

Knowing he needs encouragement, I pray for my friend, Lord. Lifting my heart to you on his behalf, may I not fail, either, to reach my hand to his—just as you are holding mine.

Wait on the Lord: be of good courage, and he shall strengthen thine heart: wait, I say, on the Lord.

—Psalm 27:14

You call me to courage, Lord, but incrementally, as a child emboldened to walk along placing each small foot in larger footprints. As once I followed my father or mother, I now follow you. I know the path marked out this way, following you step by careful step, is the only path that leads to safety.

Whate'er my fears or foes suggest,
You are my hope, my joy, my rest.
My heart shall feel your love and raise
my cheerful voice to sing your praise.
—Isaac Watts

If ye have faith as a grain of mustard seed, ye shall say unto this mountain, Remove hence to yonder place; and it shall remove; and nothing shall be impossible unto you.

—Matthew 17:20

When a task requiring faith confronts us, voices around us may say, "It can't be done." The voice may even come from within us, and we may want to quit before we start. But if we hold on to faith, we can succeed, no matter what the critics say.

No matter what my ears may hear,
Or what my eyes may see,
There's nothing for me to fear, Lord:
You're always here with me.

I called upon the Lord in distress:
the Lord answered me, and
set me in a large place.

—Psalm 118:5

When I feel my control slipping, Lord, I know I only have to call on you for encouragement, direction, and guidance to get your loving assistance.

Dear Lord,

My financial demands exceed the resources I have. The pressure I feel to do something, even if it's unwise, is building, and I fear I will cave in and make a decision I will regret. Help me trust you. Preserve my integrity and show me your way of dealing with this situation.

Amen.

For ye have not received the spirit of bondage again to fear; but ye have received the Spirit of adoption, whereby we cry, Abba, Father.

—Romans 8:15

God can help you do the thing you fear to do.

There is no fear in love; but perfect love casteth out fear.

—1 John 4:18

No matter how deep a rut we dig ourselves into, the arms of God are long enough to lift us up into a newer life free from struggle. No matter how dark a tunnel we crawl into, the love of God is strong enough to reach in and guide us toward a brighter life, free from fear.

In God I will praise his word, in God I have put my trust; I will not fear what flesh can do unto me.

—Psalm 56:4

Lord,

Help me trust you enough to tear down the walls of fear and doubt.

Amen.

You are the mighty wind,
That lifts me up on high,
When I am weak and weary,
And without the strength to fly.
You are the mighty fortress,
That keeps me free from fear,
And shelters me in kindness,
With your tender, loving care.

Deliver me out of the mire,
and let me not sink.

—Psalm 69:14

No matter the worries I have, small or large, you, O God, are there ahead of me with promises of help and support that relieve me and free me from getting stuck in the mire of my fear. I am grateful.

God of All Comfort,

I know that with you by my side I am never alone. Your love casts out all fear, doubt, and uncertainty. Your presence emboldens and empowers me. You are the light that leads me to safety again.

Amen.

And as he lay and slept under a juniper tree, behold, then an angel touched him, and said unto him, Arise and eat.

—1 Kings 19:5

God has sent angels to his people on Earth throughout eternity. Some brought messages of hope, others gave warning. Some angels helped still a fearful heart or encourage the downtrodden, like the angel who brought Elijah food when he was exhausted and despairing.

Dear God,

I blew it. Give me courage to admit my mistake, apologize, and go on. Keep me from getting stuck in denial, despair, and, worst of all, fear of trying again. In your remolding hands, God of grace, failures can become feedback and mistakes can simply be lessons in what doesn't work. Remind me that perfection means "suited to the task," not "without mistakes." There's a world of difference.

Amen.

Lord,

You know that lately I have been struggling just to get through the next hour, minute, second. Be merciful to me in my weakness and bring me strength and encouragement through the angels you send, faithful messengers of your compassion and comfort.

Amen.

O God, My Comforter and Guide,

I get discouraged, and feel overwhelmed,
which makes me even more discouraged.
Lead me beyond negative thoughts
and useless circles of worry to a
renewed frame of mind. Work your
miracle of transformation in me.

Amen.

Let us therefore follow after the things which make for peace, and things wherewith one may edify another.

—Romans 14:19

Encouragement through friends and family lifts my heart just as sunshine turns roses skyward. May their love inspire me to stretch my soul toward the warmth and nurture of your radiant affection for me.

Dear God,

A call, a note, and a handclasp from a friend are simple and seemingly insignificant. Yet you inspire these gifts from people we have a special affection for. These cherished acts of friendship nudge aside doubts about who we are when we feel low and encourage our hearts in a way that lifts our spirits. Thank you for the friends you have given us.

Amen.

Know therefore that the Lord thy God, he is God, the faithful God, which keepeth covenant and mercy with them that love him and keep his commandments to a thousand generations.

—Deuteronomy 7:9

Dear God,

I pray today to have more faith in my own abilities. I sometimes sell myself short and don't go out on a limb, afraid to fail at something even if I really want to try it. I let doubt scare me away and talk myself out of things, sure I don't have what it takes to make them happen. Then I regret never having gone after my dreams or feeling accomplished. I know that you have faith in me, but how do I find that faith for myself? Help me to recognize my own worth and strength, and to see that I am far more capable than I imagine myself to be. Help me to reach above and beyond where I am to get to where I want to be and to feel happy and fulfilled again.

Amen.

Lord,

You're never missing in action—you're with me all the time, everywhere, without fail. Please keep this knowledge in the forefront of my mind today so I'll be encouraged and emboldened to move through each challenge without feeling intimidated, fearful, or ashamed. May I always be kept safe because of your keeping power at work in my life.

In your name, I pray.

But ye shall receive power, after that the Holy Ghost is come upon you: and ye shall be witnesses unto me.

—Acts 1:8

We will know when it's time to make our stand. God will speak to us a little louder, a little stronger. The whisper within will become a mighty roar, as we are encouraged to step out in faith and be the person God meant us to be.

There is none holy as the Lord: for there is none beside thee: neither is there any rock like our God.

—1 Samuel 2:2

When the world rocks you off your center, hold fast to God to bring you back to harmony and balance. When life pulls the rug out from under you, jump and land square on the foundation of God's love for you. When all seems lost, God will help you find your way again.

Lord God,

I am about to throw in the towel! I can't go on without your strength to get me over the edge and into the light again. Help me remember why I chose these goals and dreams to begin with, God. Keep me strong to the finish!

Amen.

And when they had prayed, the place was shaken where they were assembled together; and they were all filled with the Holy Ghost, and they spake the word of God with boldness.

—Acts 4:31

I pray today for a clear path, a strong wind at my back pushing me forward, and the courage of a lion to step into greatness. I am afraid and uncomfortable, but with you I can begin the journey of a thousand miles—with one bold step.

Lord,

A friend is going through an incredibly difficult time. Sometimes even well-meaning words can grate on raw nerves, and I don't want to say the wrong thing or, in trying to make things better, minimize her pain. When I am with her, please give me the right words to say at the right time—whether they are words of encouragement, commiseration, or understanding. And if what she needs is simply a comforting hug while she cries, let me be present with her. Sometimes silence is the best gift we have to offer.

Amen.

He that receiveth a prophet in the name of a prophet shall receive a prophet's reward; and he that receiveth a righteous man in the name of a righteous man shall receive a righteous man's reward.

—Matthew 10:41

After Jesus taught his disciples to pray, he sends them out to gather lost sheep, ministering to those who had lost their way. Here he promises to reward those who helped his disciples and received their teaching. Is there some servant of God whom you can encourage today, by listening or helping? If so, there is a promised reward.

FORGIVENESS
in Times of Strife

Blessed is he whose transgression is forgiven, whose sin is covered.

—Psalm 32:1

Forgiveness is the central virtue in God's treasure chest—God's forgiveness of us and our forgiveness of others and ourselves. At times we find that forgiveness comes very easily, even for grievous and painful hurts. But many times, we seem powerless to forgive, no matter how hard we try. This is when God's forgiving grace has the opportunity to touch and change us and then be extended to others through our example.

Those who forgive most
shall be most forgiven.

—Philip James Bailey

He that cannot forgive others, breaks the bridge over which he himself must pass if he would ever reach heaven, for everyone has need to be forgiven.

—George Herbert

Forgiveness is a supernatural response to being wronged. Would we know what forgiveness is if God had not shown us by first forgiving us? It seems highly unlikely. That's why real forgiveness—the kind that God extends to us—can only come through God's grace. In our own strength, we may try to forgive someone over and over again, only to call to mind the offense later (for perhaps the hundredth time). But when we ask God to open our hearts, he fills them with his love and makes us capable of full forgiveness.

Hide thy face from my sins, and blot out all mine iniquities.

—Psalm 51:9

Lord,

Sometimes my past rises up to haunt me—or worse yet, to bite me. These are the real-world consequences of poor choices I've made. But even though I'm reminded of them because of the cause-and-effect nature of things, once I confess them to you and receive your forgiveness, they are erased from your record book. So even when I'm reminded of my old sins in one way or another, help me to quickly let go of any guilt or shame that rears its ugly head. While consequences may linger, your forgiveness is complete. Thank you for that eternal reality.

Amen.

In all this Job sinned not, nor charged God foolishly.

—Job 1:22

God,

When things go wrong, we often blame you first. Forgive us for even considering that you would deliberately hurt one of your very own children. What could you possibly have to gain? Thank you for your presence, and please forgive our many sins.

Amen.

Therefore if any man be in Christ, he is a new creature: old things are passed away; behold, all things are become new.

—2 Corinthians 5:17

When it seems that scarcely a day ends by saying, "If only I could do it over. I regret what I said, did, or didn't do," the God of fresh starts is eager to make things right. All we need to say is, "Forgive me for today, and show me how to redeem myself for tomorrow."

Lord, I confess to you,
Sadly, my sin;
All I am, I tell to you,
All I have been.
Purge all my sin away,
Wash clean my soul this day;
Lord, make me clean.
Then all is peace and light this soul within;
Thus shall I walk with you,
Loved though unseen.
Leaning on you, my God,
Guided along the road,
Nothing between!
—Horatius Bonar

Lord,

I feel angry at so many people. Often I think my life would be peaceful if only they would just do the right thing. I convince myself they are robbing me of peace, but at this moment I know it's my choice to let go of anger and embrace peace. Staying angry at them for not living up to my expectations doesn't solve any problems—it just creates new ones. Please help me to remember that "the wrath of man worketh not the righteousness of God" (James 1:20)—in me or in those I'm staying angry at. Give me strength to release them—over and over again if need be—so I can go back to that serene, tranquil place called "peace."

In Jesus's name. Amen.

God,

When I've been hurt, my anger and resentment feel justified. Yet I know that my lack of forgiveness hurts me as much as it hurts the one who hurt me. I need your help with forgiveness. Help me forgive anyone who has ever wounded me, however slight or great the hurt. Forgive me both the offenses I did on purpose and the ways I hurt others without realizing it. Whenever possible, let me know how to make amends to those I have hurt. Help me accept forgiveness from others and graciously offer my own forgiveness, for this is the way that leads to life.

Amen.

He healeth the broken in heart,
and bindeth up their wounds.

—Psalm 147:3

When someone breaks our heart, we mourn, we grieve, and we feel the pain of rejection. We pray to God for healing and relief. And then we pick up the pieces and, with God's help and guidance, rebuild a heart that is even stronger, more resilient, and ready to love again.

But if ye forgive not men their trespasses, neither will your Father forgive your trespasses.

—Matthew 6:15

Lord,

I know it is your will for us to forgive those who do us wrong, and I know that once we do, everything goes so much more smoothly in our lives. We forgive because you first forgave us, and I'm starting to understand that. Help me to forgive, Lord. Take away the hurt and betrayal, and leave only your peace.

Amen.

The Lord hath spoken peace to my soul,
He hath blessed me abundantly,
Hath pardoned my sins;
He hath shown me great mercy
and saved me by his love.
I will sing of his goodness
and mercy while I live,
And ever, forever will praise his holy name.
O how sweet to trust in God,
And to know your sins forgiven,
To believe his precious word,
And be guided by his love.
Therefore goodness and mercy,
Shall follow me all the days of my life.
Amen.

—C.E. Leslie

And when he saw their faith, he said unto him, Man, thy sins are forgiven thee.

—Luke 5:20

O God,

I am guilty of transgressions that make me ashamed, and I fear you'll leave me. Yet have you ever refused to forgive those who ask? Why would I be different? Reassured, I accept forgiveness and will share it with those who need it from me.

Amen.

Search me, O God, and know my heart: try me, and know my thoughts: And see if there be any wicked way in me, and lead me in the way everlasting.

—Psalm 139:23–24

It's hard, Lord, to reveal my heart to you, though it's the thing I most want to do. Remind me in this dialogue that you already know what is within me. You wait—O thank you!—hoping for the gift of my willingness to acknowledge the good you already see and the bad you've long forgotten.

God is our refuge and strength, a very present help in trouble.

—Psalm 46:1

Lord,

We should not just turn to you in times of trouble, we should run to you. Where else can we find both shelter and consolation? Where else can we feel both completely safe and unconditionally loved? Thank you for opening your arms to us whenever we need to run into them. Help us learn to run to you at the first sign of trouble. You are an unfailing refuge.

Amen.

The story is told that someone asked Martin Luther (1483–1546) if he "felt" that he had been forgiven. His reply:

"No, but I'm as sure as there's a God in Heaven. For feelings come, and feelings go, and feelings are deceiving. My warrant is the Word of God, naught else is worth believing."

Whither shall I go from thy spirit? or whither shall I flee from thy presence?

—Psalm 139:7

Lord,

You know me. Sometimes, that thought is intimidating. I don't want you to see all my flaws and foibles! I become discouraged by the thought of how petty I must seem to you, how earthly my concerns. I think that if you truly know me, you'll think me unworthy of your love. But I know you do love me! You alone can both fully know me and fully love me. I thank you for that incredible gift.

Amen.

Lord, why is it that we mothers feel embarrassed when our youngsters misbehave in public? They are just being children, yet our cheeks burn with shame when they are less than perfect. Then, to cover our embarrassment, we treat them unfairly or embarrass them.

Forgive me when I react to my children in a less-than-loving way, Father. You never withhold your love from me. Grant me the wisdom and understanding to deal with problems before they get out of hand, and to avoid the anger that clouds my good judgment.

Childhood passes so quickly. I don't want to spend it scolding and reprimanding. Show me how to deal with my children in loving-kindness, as you do, and to let them know how much they mean to me.

A new commandment I give unto you, That ye love one another; as I have loved you, that ye also love one another.

—John 13:34

God,

Teach me to walk in love today. With the stressful and hectic nature of life, I find myself giving in to anger, unkindness, and even hatred, and that is not how I want to live or behave. Help me turn to a loving solution for every problem, and to stand in love even when I am surrounded by negativity and confusion. Show me how to always depend on your love, even if at times my own capacity to love others fails me. I ask that I always try to be a loving channel of your presence, and that in the times when I am failing, you come to my aid and remind me of the precious power of love and how much it is needed in this world. Thank you, God.

Amen.

I say unto you, Love your enemies, bless them that curse you, do good to them that hate you, and pray for them which despitefully use you, and persecute you.

—Matthew 5:44

We know that revenge will settle nothing at this point. It will only leave us with an emptier feeling than before. Heal the pain in our hurts over this injustice, and somehow, as impossible as it now seems, bring us to the place of blessing our enemies and extending the one thing that keeps saving our own lives: your forgiveness.

We're stained, like a paint rag, by troubles we caused ourselves, Lord. Red, the color of lost temper and rudeness. Green, envy of others who have it easier and more of it. Blue, the shade of despair over something we could change. Yellow, of cowardly running. Rearrange our unsightly smudges into glorious rainbows through your gift of forgiveness.

I came not to call the righteous,
but sinners to repentance.

—Luke 5:32

My guard is constant and vigilant, protecting me against the next episode of my humanness. I know to err is human, but why so often? Peace only comes, God of wholeness, through reassurance that with you, mistakes, errors—even disasters—can yield treasures. I am so grateful.

If I have wounded any soul today,
If I have caused one foot to go astray,
If I have walked in my own willful way,
Dear Lord, forgive!
If I have uttered idle words or vain,
If I have turned aside from want or pain,
Lest I myself shall suffer
through the strain,
Dear Lord, forgive!
Forgive the sins I have confessed to thee;
Forgive the secret sins I do not see;
O guide me, love me and my keeper be,
Dear Lord, Amen.

—C. Maude Battersby

Take my hand, precious Lord, as I take on the role of peacemaker. Lead me through the minefield of broken relationships between my child and another.

Make me sensitive to hurt feelings on both sides, and fill me with the compassion and understanding to negotiate the delicate situation fairly.

Give both children an appreciation for the friendship they have enjoyed, and make them understand the need for apology and forgiveness. Help them to put the past behind them, start fresh, and build a new relationship.

It is painful to see misery on these young children's faces, Lord. Use me to help them mend this friendship and restore the sunshine.

We have redemption through his blood, the forgiveness of sins, according to the riches of his grace.

—Ephesians 1:7

God of Second Chances,

There is in your grace insufficient evidence to prove my latest setback is a failure. Even if it is, with you, failure is never final but an opportunity to learn and grow. When I goof, as I am prone to do, help me from doubling the problem by failing to take advantage of your redemption.

Amen.

Be it known unto you therefore, men and brethren, that through this man is preached unto you the forgiveness of sins: And by him all that believe are justified from all things, from which ye could not be justified by the law of Moses.

—Acts 13:38–39

God,

I ask in prayer for your forgiveness. I've not been the most loving and kind person lately, and I've treated people terribly as a result. I plan to reach out to each and every one of them and ask their forgiveness, but first I come to you in hopes that you will help me be a better person, a more loving and caring friend, and someone who treats others as I'd like to be treated. Please take away the defects in me that cause me to do harm to others, and strengthen the good qualities I have. I am a loving person, but when life backs me into a corner, I know I can be awful. Please forgive me and empower me to make better choices in the future and be the person you want me to be.

Amen.

O God, whose nature and property is ever to have mercy and to forgive, receive our humble petitions; and though we be tied and bound with the chain of our sins, yet let the pitifulness of thy great mercy loose us; for the honor of Jesus Christ, our mediator, and advocate.

—St. Gregory

But that ye may know that the Son of man hath power upon earth to forgive sins, (he said unto the sick of the palsy,) I say unto thee, Arise, and take up thy couch, and go into thine house.

—Luke 5:24

Dear God,

I don't come in prayer to you to ask for total forgiveness, even though I know you do forgive me my sins and mistakes. I ask that in addition to your merciful grace, you also help me to learn from my experience and glean wisdom from my interactions with the people I need to forgive, or from whom I need forgiveness. Without this understanding, I fear I will repeat the same patterns in the future. Forgive me, God, then help me to forgive. But then, please, help me to increase my wisdom and come to a place in life where I don't keep repeating the same mistakes over and over again.

Amen.

I need to ask someone for forgiveness. Part of me wants to brush off and minimize what I did, to say that what I did wasn't so bad—maybe the other person didn't even notice! But I don't want to start to walk astray in little things. God, give me strength to do this properly and offer a genuine, loving apology.

Blessed are the merciful: for they shall obtain mercy.

—Matthew 5:7

For those times when friends or family members have forgiven me when I wronged them, I offer thanks and ask your blessings upon them. They taught me about how powerful mercy can be. O merciful God, let me in turn be merciful to others.

Forgive, O Lord, for thy dear Son
The ill that I this day have done.
That with the world, myself, and thee
I, ere I sleep, at peace may be.
—Traditional evening prayer

HOPE
in Times of Despair

In hope that sends a shining ray
Far down the future's broad'ning way,
In peace that only thou canst give,
With thee, O Master, let me live.
—Washington Gladden

Abide in me, and I in you. As the branch cannot bear fruit of itself, except it abide in the vine; no more can ye, except ye abide in me.

—John 15:4

God,

Teach us to know, that it is exactly at the point of our deepest despair that you are closest. For at those times we can finally admit we have wandered in the dark, without a clue. Yet you have been there with us all along. Thank you for your abiding presence.

Amen.

Therefore my heart is glad, and my glory rejoiceth: my flesh also shall rest in hope.

—Psalm 16:9

We can take a lesson from the precious water lily. For no matter what outside force or pressure is put upon the lily, it always rises back to the water's surface again to feel the nurturing sunlight upon its leaves and petals. We must be like the lily, steadfast and true in the face of every difficulty, that we too may rise above our problems and feel God's light upon our faces again.

Stop moaning and asking,
"Why, God, why?"

There is always a meaningful reason.

Stop whining and pleading,
"When, God, when?"

For good things will arrive in due season.

We are promised that God's never early,

But neither is God ever late.

All the blessings we wish will come to us

When we learn to have
faith while we wait.

When I am lost and discouraged,

And there seems to be no hope in sight,

I turn my cares over to the
God of my heart,

And his love lets my spirit take flight.

And God shall wipe away all tears from their eyes; and there shall be no more death, neither sorrow, nor crying, neither shall there be any more pain: for the former things are passed away. And he that sat upon the throne said, Behold, I make all things new.

—Revelation 21:4–5

Like a speed bump in a parking lot, a decision lies in our path, placed there by God to remind us hope is a choice. Choosing to live as people of hope is not to diminish or belittle pain and suffering or lie about evil's reality. Rather it is to cling to God's promise that he will make all things new.

O Lord,

When I see terrible, fearful events—
explosions destroying whole buildings,
droughts that turn crops to dust,
storms devastating all in their path—
then I turn to you. And you are always
here, listening, caring, and waiting
for all of us to reach out to you.

Amen.

Be of good courage, and he shall strengthen your heart, all ye that hope in the Lord.

—Psalm 31:24

Just when all seems hopeless, prayer lifts us like a wave on the ocean. A sturdy craft, prayer doesn't hide from pain, but uses it like the force of the sea to move us to a new place of insight, patience, courage, and sympathy. Always, it is God's hand beneath the surface holding us up.

O God, our help in ages past,
Our hope for years to come;
Be thou our guide while life shall last,
And our eternal home.
Under the shadow of thy throne,
Still may we dwell secure;
Sufficient is thine arm alone,
And our defense is sure.
—Isaac Watts

Lord,

I am weary and cannot find my way. The nights seem endless and thick with a fog that engulfs my spirit, but I have faith in you, my Lord and my light. Faith that you will help me take another step when I feel I can no longer walk on my own. Faith that you will be the beacon of hope that guides my way through the darkness. Faith that this, too, shall pass and that I will know joy again.

Amen.

In his neck remaineth strength, and sorrow is turned into joy before him.

—Job 41:22

Traumatic events leave a void in our souls that only a closer relationship with God can fill. By asking God to help us through hard times, we truly come to understand that we are never alone and that sadness is only a precursor to joy and pain a precursor to healing.

Then they cried unto the Lord in their trouble, and he saved them out of their distresses. He brought them out of darkness and the shadow of death, and brake their bands in sunder.

—Psalm 107:13–14

Life, once filled with sunlight and promise, has been colored by loss and is now all storm and shadow. Use my tears, Lord, as the showers needed to bring rainbows. Shine your love on me as the sun; lift my eyes so I can see even the smallest curves of hope in the dark (but lightening) sky.

Strengthen ye the weak hands, and confirm the feeble knees. Say to them that are of a fearful heart, Be strong, fear not: behold, your God will come with vengeance, even God with a recompence; he will come and save you.

—Isaiah 35:3–4

When the despair that comes with the pain of a loss immobilizes us and makes us feel powerless, God gives us the inner fortitude and grace we need to get up, get over the suffering, and get on with our lives.

Abide with me,
Fast falls the eventide;
The darkness deepens;
Lord, with me abide!
When other helpers fail
And comforts flee,
Help of the helpless,
O abide with me.
I need thy presence
Every passing hour;
What but thy grace
Can foil the tempter's power?
Who like thyself,
My guide and stay can be?
Through cloud and sunshine,
Lord, abide, with me.
—Henry F. Lyte

And the dove came in to him in the evening; and, lo, in her mouth was an olive leaf pluckt off: so Noah knew that the waters were abated from off the earth.

—Genesis 8:11

When hope seems gone, I spy doves like those God sent Noah to assure him the storm was subsiding. Doves of inspiration, knowledge, understanding; doves in the shape of those not letting me travel alone. I'm energized for the rest of the journey. Land is in sight.

O God of our salvation; who art the confidence of all the ends of the earth, and of them that are afar off upon the sea: Which by his strength setteth fast the mountains; being girded with power: Which stilleth the noise of the seas, the noise of their waves, and the tumult of the people.

—Psalm 65:5–7

No matter what is going on outside of us, hope is that quiet whisper within that gives us the strength and courage to keep going. The ways of the world may be chaotic, loud, and distracting, but we can keep a sense of inner calm when our hope is centered in God's eternal presence. Hope is our anchor to the rock of God's love when we feel tossed and turned upon the waves of life.

When life's winds toss me,
Upon the waves of uncertainty and doubt,
And when the tempest beats me,
Upon rocks of guilt and self-pity,
When my pitiful heart yearns
for love I cannot find,
When the darkness seems darker,
And the night longer,
Some unseen hand reaches down,
And with a strength and tenderness
I cannot comprehend,
Pulls me back into the light.

Holy Spirit,

Help me live one day at a time so that I
may meet each day's challenges with grace,
courage, and hope. Shelter me from the
fears of the future and the anguish of the
past. Keep my mind and heart focused
on the present, where the true gifts of
happiness and healing are to be found.

Amen.

Why art thou cast down, O my soul? and why art thou disquieted within me? hope in God: for I shall yet praise him, who is the health of my countenance, and my God.

—Psalm 43:5

Many times I feel that I have the right to be downcast. But God's Word says that we should not be downcast because we have an amazing hope through him. If I focus on this hope, joy will enter my spirit, and my negative emotions will disperse.

Give to the winds thy fears,
Hope and be undismayed,
God hears thy sighs and counts thy tears,
God shall lift up thy head.
Through waves and clouds and storms,
He gently clears thy way.
Wait thou his time; so shall this night
Soon end in joyous day.
Let us in life, death,
They steadfast truth declare
And publish with our latest breath
Thy love and guardian care.

—Paul Gerhardt, translated
by John Wesley

Are not five sparrows sold for two farthings, and not one of them is forgotten before God?

—Luke 12:6

Lord,

Sometimes we struggle with an issue for longer than necessary because we foolishly think it isn't worth your time. We know that everything that exists, everything that lives and breathes, everything that happens does so with your full knowledge. Give us hearts and minds that are open to this amazing truth, that we have hope in both large and small matters.

Amen.

Dear Lord,

It's hard to be grateful for difficult times. Help me to see my trials as an opportunity to grow and change. Help me reach out to others who are suffering their own difficult times. Thank you, Jesus, for the chance to know you better through my suffering. Help me remember and be grateful for the suffering you endured to help me. Let me find the bright side of every trial and the strength to be grateful for the test.

Amen.

Hope is the best possession. None
are completely wretched but
those who are without hope.

—William Hazlitt

Without Christ there is no hope.

—Charles Spurgeon

The people which sat in darkness saw great light; and to them which sat in the region and shadow of death light is sprung up.

—Matthew 4:16

We wander like children lost in a cave, perilously close to the edge of despair. Unable to see where we're going, we crouch in fear rather than risk falling while searching for an exit. Nudge us beyond fear; send us guides who have traveled dark passages before.

Life is not easy; in fact, some days, even arising to face the day is a truly daunting task. Because sin entered the world and corrupted God's perfect design, we may find ourselves bruised like fragile reeds by the painful effects of a broken world. If we allow ourselves to stay in our broken state without relying on the powerful source of God's comfort, peace, and love, we might even find ourselves as hopeless as a smoldering wick about to lose its flame.

The state of hopelessness is dangerous; it is one of the worst places to allow ourselves to dwell. However, God knows our heartache, and he understands our suffering. When we have been bruised in this world, he offers us healing. We may never understand why we have to encounter heartbreaking experiences, but we can hold securely to the truth that God's justice is certain. He will heat our hearts with the flame of his joy again.

As I trust in you, God, I know you will fill my life with your hope. That hope will transcend into every area of my soul, and beautiful buds of joy and peace will begin to grow. I want your joy and peace to be obvious in my life.

I'm tired of pretending to be joyful and acting like I'm peaceful. I desire those fruits to grow naturally, out of the wellspring of hope in my heart.

Prod me to trust you at all times, Lord, and to rely on your Word. I know that my joy and peace are complete in you, and I have hope that you can work in me despite my weaknesses. I'm done with putting my hope into the changing tides of this world. I'm ready to put all of my hope in you, so real fruits of joy and peace can grow.

Hope deferred maketh the heart sick: but when the desire cometh, it is a tree of life.

—Proverbs 13:12

We all know the sting of being heartsick. Loss, unrequited love, unfulfilled expectations—any of these can lead to the feeling of our heart literally being sick. The passage above tells us that it is actually deferring, or putting off, hope that truly makes our hearts sick. God knows the pain we experience in this life. He knows how to comfort us. If we cling to hope and turn to God, despite all that life may throw at us, we are sure to find ourselves filled with peace and joy.

I falter where I firmly trod,
And falling with my weight of cares
Upon the great world's altar stairs
That slope through darkness up to God,
I stretch lame hands of faith, and grope,
And gather dust and chaff, and call
To what I feel is Lord of all,
And faintly trust the larger hope.
—Alfred, Lord Tennyson

And, behold, there came a man named Jairus, and he was a ruler of the synagogue: and he fell down at Jesus' feet, and besought him that he would come into his house: For he had one only daughter, about twelve years of age, and she lay a dying.

—Luke 8:41–42

All of us face difficult hours in our lives—hours when in tears we fall to our knees and plead something similar to what this father uttered. Just as the Lord stood ready to help this father, so he is ready to assist us today.

For thou art my hope, O Lord God: thou art my trust from my youth.

—Psalm 71:5

If I put my hope in people, I am often disappointed. If I put my hope in circumstances, I am often let down. But when I put my hope in God, I am always taken care of. God is my rock and my hope, in him is a firm foundation from which I live my life. I may not always get all my hoped-for prayers answered the way I expect, but I get them answered the way God wants me to.

Now the God of hope fill you with all joy and peace in believing, that ye may abound in hope, through the power of the Holy Ghost.

—Romans 15:13

The promise of hope fills the heart with a new perspective, and the eyes with a new vision. Darkness begins to lift, showing the path we could not see before, and a way out of our pain and suffering. The promise of hope opens doors we were certain were closed, and reveals solutions that evaded us. Hope is a key that unlocks the way to the blessings of God around us.

But let us, who are of the day, be sober, putting on the breastplate of faith and love; and for an helmet, the hope of salvation.

—1 Thessalonians 5:8

I cannot see the light, but I know it is just up ahead. I cannot find the way out, but I know that my path is leading me there. I cannot solve the problem, but I know the solution is on its way. I know these things because of my faith in God, who has never failed me, and never will.

The blessing of the Lord, it maketh rich, and he addeth no sorrow with it.

—Proverbs 10:22

An attitude of gratitude can help you get through even the roughest of times. Focusing on God's blessings helps you realize just how loved you are. It isn't about ignoring all the things that go wrong or bring you suffering, but always remembering to look for the blessing in the lesson, and the silver lining in the dark clouds above.

And hope maketh not ashamed; because the love of God is shed abroad in our hearts by the Holy Ghost which is given unto us.

—Romans 5:5

Our confidence, even our boldness, comes from the love of God. By his Spirit, his love simply shines in our lives and encourages others. How can we be ashamed of it? How can we hide it? There is nothing more precious. And there is nothing more true. This is our great expectation and hope, that we are loved by the creator and ruler of the universe who gave us his Spirit. That makes today, and every day, a good day.

PEACE

in Times of Anxiety

For he is our peace, who hath made both one.

—Ephesians 2:14

Peace describes the state of being we all desire to have. The word "peace" brings to mind "the absence of war." It evokes images of people getting along with one another and living together in harmony. A similar sense comes from having inner peace: a quality of internal rest and calm. But neither kind of peace can be had without paying the price for it: We must release everything to God. We know that we've acquired true peace if, when things are chaotic all around us, we can be calm and trust in the one of whom the scriptures say, "He is our peace..."

These things I have spoken unto you, that in me ye might have peace. In the world ye shall have tribulation: but be of good cheer; I have overcome the world.

—John 16:33

Sometimes we believe our souls can only be at peace if there is no outer turmoil. The wonder of God's peace is that even when the world around us is in confusion and our emotions are in a whirl, underneath it all we can know his peace.

And the very God of peace sanctify you wholly; and I pray God your whole spirit and soul and body be preserved blameless unto the coming of our Lord Jesus Christ.

—1 Thessalonians 5:23

Speak, move, act in peace, as if you were in prayer. In truth, this is prayer.

—François de Salignac
de la Mothe-Fénelon

My people shall dwell in a peaceable habitation, and in sure dwellings, and in quiet resting places.

—Isaiah 32:18

God,

When life feels like a ride that won't let us off, remind us that you are waiting for us to reach up to you. And when we finally do, thank you for being there to lift us to peace and safety.

Amen.

And I will pray the Father, and he shall give you another Comforter, that he may abide with you for ever.

—John 14:16

One of the best things you can say to a friend is simply, "I'll be there for you." Nothing to do, nothing to prove, just the assurance of your presence when they need you. That's exactly what God tells us time and time again in the Bible. He will be there for us.

For in the time of trouble he shall hide me in his pavilion: in the secret of his tabernacle shall he hide me; he shall set me up upon a rock.

—Psalm 27:5

Lord,

The clamor of my life is unbearable. People pressing in on all sides. Decisions crying out to be made. Problems needing to be solved. I don't want to get out of bed in the morning. I want to hide, to escape. Please help me!

Amen.

Lord, dismiss us with thy blessing,
Hope, and comfort from above;
Let us each, thy peace possessing,
Triumph in redeeming love.
—Robert Hawker

Dear God,

Everything in my life lately seems to be going wrong. People are uncaring. Things I've worked hard for don't seem to be coming to fruition. Everyone needs my time and attention and I feel so tired and overwhelmed and stressed. I ask today in prayer for peace, for serenity. I don't ask for a removal of my problems, but for the power and fortitude to deal with them as they arise from a place of calm and stillness within. I know that you can provide me that kind of amazing, unerring peace. Be the rock upon which I can take comfort and rest when the world spins out of control all around me. Be my peace everlasting.

Amen.

Casting all your care upon him; for he careth for you.

—1 Peter 5:7

Our worries are hard to dismiss, Lord. They seem to grow bigger and bigger until they take over our lives. Please help us conquer them, one at a time. Your reassurance is welcome.

Amen.

Peace I leave with you, my peace I give unto you: not as the world giveth, give I unto you. Let not your heart be troubled, neither let it be afraid.

—John 14:27

Yes, Father in heaven, often have we found that the world cannot give us peace, O but make us feel that thou art able to give us peace; let us know the truth of thy promise: that the whole world may not be able to take away thy peace.

—Søren Kierkegaard

Mercy unto you, and peace, and love, be multiplied.

—Jude 1:2

His love is wider than our worries, longer than our loneliness, stronger than our sorrows, deeper than our doubts, and higher than our hostilities. This is why valleys are so wide, rivers so long, winds so strong, oceans so deep, and the sky is so high—with these, we can have a picture of the wonder of his love.

God,

I look around sometimes and see no reason to love my life. My eyes are so often focused on the negative things—the challenges and obstacles and the frustrations of trying to do the best I can all the time. Please don't ever let me lose my ability to dig deep to that special place within where love lives. Please help me always keep my love alive, even when I am exhausted and defeated. Let your love remind me that I have the choice to go a little deeper, to move beyond the pain and the annoyances, and to find that calm and serene well within that never runs dry.

Amen.

Like the littered house in the aftermath of the holidays, my soul is overcrowded. What, I worry, do I need to be a good parent?

Guide my sorting: Keep humor; toss battles of will. Keep tolerance and imagination; toss inflexibility and overreactive fear. Keep respect and acceptance of kids just as they are today; toss supermom lists and myths and others' expectations.

Guided by you, O God, my sorting will continue as I toss out useless worrying habits.

Be perfect, be of good comfort, be of one mind, live in peace; and the God of love and peace shall be with you.

—2 Corinthians 13:11

Where there is peace, God is.

—George Herbert

Lord God,

When you say something, it is as good as done. It may not take place in the timing that I'd imagine or wish, but you are true to your word without fail. So when you tell me not to be anxious—but rather to pray and you will give me your peace—I'll just do that. When you say that you forgive me when I confess my sin, I'll believe that. When you tell me that I'm your child and that you rejoice over me, I'll take pleasure in that. Whatever you say, I'll not doubt it. Thank you for your great and precious promises and for your absolute trustworthiness.

Amen.

Gentle Lord,

For the first time I listened to myself as I frantically got the family ready for school. In my frustration, I barked out orders and hurled angry words in every direction. No wonder the children are in a grumpy mood. I know it's time I changed my tune.

Grant me more patience, Lord, and teach me how to guard my tongue. Make my words soothing and sweet like the honeycomb, so my children can arrive at school in a calmer, happier frame of mind. Teach me the lesson, Lord, that pleasant words get better results.

Amen.

Like a river glorious is
God's perfect peace,

Over all victorious in
its bright increase;

Perfect, yet it floweth
fuller every day,

Perfect, yet it groweth
deeper all the way.

Ev'ry joy or trial falleth from above,

Traced upon our dial by
the sun of love;

We may trust him fuller
all for us to do

They who trust him wholly
find him wholly true.

Stayed upon Jehovah,
hearts are fully blest—

Finding, as he promised,
perfect peace and rest.

—Frances Ridley Havergal

Therefore being justified by faith, we have peace with God through our Lord Jesus Christ.

—Romans 5:1

Every day I'm exposed to a world whose values don't jibe with yours, Lord. I am in need of constant reminders to not get caught up in notions that money, power, status, and physical appearance are of utmost importance. While the movers and shakers of society endorse such things as necessary for a fulfilling existence, you say that faithfulness to you is where real life is lived out and lasting inner peace is achieved. O Lord, help me when I'm tempted to believe that I can prevail in life by being seen as "strong" in ways that ultimately don't matter to you.

He maketh the storm a calm, so that the waves thereof are still.

—Psalm 107:29

Calm me enough, O Lord, to breathe deeply and restoratively despite my racing heart, pounding headache, and generally fatigued body and mind. Prayer restores me in the presence of all that threatens to undo me, which I name to you now.

Lord,

I try to remain calm and loving, but sometimes I get so upset with my kids that I want to explode. I'm not proud of the hurtful words that come out of my mouth, but I can't seem to stop them.

Father, you are the God of peace. Fill me with your quiet spirit. Teach me to get control of my anger before lashing out at the children. Prevent me from blaming them instead of calmly stating the reasons for my anger.

Remind me that my aim is to soothe not to stir up anger. Give me a tongue that is soft and gentle rather than harsh and perverse so my young ones will be inspired to change their behavior.

Amen.

Before me peaceful,
Behind me peaceful,
Under me peaceful,
Over me peaceful,
All around me peaceful.

Lord,

I have seen homes where family members were continually at war with one another. I don't want our family to live like that. With your help, I have resolved to make our home a quiet place for my husband and children—a refuge from the noise and discord of the world outside.

O God of peace and contentment, you have chosen us to live together both as a family and as part of the body of Christ. We invite you now to come into our home, our hearts, and our minds, so your peace may dwell there.

Amen.

Of the increase of his government and peace there shall be no end, upon the throne of David, and upon his kingdom, to order it, and to establish it with judgment and with justice from henceforth even for ever.

—Isaiah 9:7

Life's not fair, and I stomp my foot in frustration. The powerful get more so as the rest of us shrink, dreams for peace are shattered as bullies get the upper hand, and despair is as tempting as an ice cream sundae. Help me hold on, for you are a God of justice and dreams, of turning life upside down. Let me help; thanks for listening in the meantime.

Where there is charity and wisdom,
there is neither fear nor ignorance.
Where there is patience and humility,
there is neither anger nor vexation.
Where there is poverty and joy,
there is neither greed nor avarice.
Where there is peace and meditation,
there is neither anxiety nor doubt.
—St. Francis of Assisi

Therefore I say unto you, Take no thought for your life, what ye shall eat, or what ye shall drink; nor yet for your body, what ye shall put on. Is not the life more than meat, and the body than raiment? Behold the fowls of the air: for they sow not, neither do they reap, nor gather into barns; yet your heavenly Father feedeth them.

—Matthew 6:25–26

Give the Lord your worries, and then let him keep them.

Lord,

How hard it is for us all to live in peace with one another. We all have our own ideas about how the world should be, and some topics can be polarizing. Help us to act in loving ways and to work hard to see and respect others' points of view. We all love this world and you—please help us keep this in mind and work from there. It is easy to get ahead of ourselves and lose hope; we also know, though, that you are always present, and we truly believe that anything is possible with you. We place the troubles of our world at your feet. We know you will mold them into something breathtaking.

Amen.

And the peace of God, which passeth all understanding, shall keep your hearts and minds through Christ Jesus.

—Philippians 4:7

Almighty God,

There are so many times when we come before you and simply confess, "We don't understand." Keep us from wasting time trying to make sense of the inscrutable! While we never want to stop mining your Word for gems of knowledge, help us find peace in the truths we can fathom and trust you with everything else.

Amen.

Lord,

I am overwhelmed with the whirl of activity around me. Getting the children up and dressed, making breakfast, taking them to school, doing dishes, cleaning house, running errands, fielding phone calls, meeting appointments, retrieving the kids, supervising homework, delivering them to music lessons and sports practices, dealing with calamities...how do I fit it all in? I am buckling under the weight of each day, only to find that I must get up and start all over again the next. Father, you are a God of peace and tranquility. I long to find a time to sit down and talk to you. Show me a quiet place in the midst of the frenzy, where I may commune with you, be refreshed, and know that through your strength, I can accomplish all that you have set out for me to do today.

Amen.

Drop thy still dews of quietness,
Till all our strivings cease;
Take from our souls the strain and stress,
And let our ordered lives confess
The beauty of thy peace.
—John Greenleaf Whittier

Be careful for nothing; but in every thing by prayer and supplication with thanksgiving let your requests be made known unto God.

—Philippians 4:6

Fretting produces nothing but overblown what-if scenarios in our minds. We end up suffering appetite loss when we need to be keeping up our strength and sleeplessness when we should be resting. How do we get off this treadmill of worry? We do just what this verse tells us to do: We take our big ol' bundle of fears and frets and hand them over to God. We say, "This is obviously too much for me to handle. Please help me with this situation, Lord." We know that if we do this, it will all work out for the best on God's timetable.

O God,

Who art the unsearchable abyss of peace, the ineffable sea of love, the fountain of blessings, and the bestower of affection, who sendest peace to those that receive it; open to us this day the sea of thy love, and water us with the plenteous streams from the riches of thy grace. Make us children of quietness, and heirs of peace. Enkindle in us the fire of thy love; sow in us thy fear; strengthen our weakness by thy power; bind us closely to thee and to each other in one firm bond of unity; for the sake of Jesus Christ.

—Early liturgical prayer

He shall enter into peace: they shall rest in their beds, each one walking in his uprightness.

—Isaiah 57:2

How restful it is to live in your love, Lord God! In the middle of chaos or turmoil, I remember that you are with me, and I am at peace once again. When it seems as if everything is falling apart, you hold me close in your love, and I am able to sleep at night. There is no other source of peace like belonging to you, Father.

Thank you for both rain and sun.

Thank you for both night and day.

Thank you for both quiet and noise.

Thank you for both challenges
and peaceful times.

Thank you when I have little, and
thank you when I have much.

Thank you in all times.

And when they had found him, they said unto him, All men seek for thee. And he said unto them, Let us go into the next towns, that I may preach there also: for therefore came I forth.

—Mark 1:37–38

Jesus had to balance the need for private prayer and public ministry. So do those of us who follow him! Time spent alone with God renews us spiritually, but we are also called to share God's words and God's love with others. If we feel drained and irritated, it may point us towards a spiritual need to be fulfilled. If we're feeling anxious or restless in our prayer lives, it may be because we have energy that's not being carried outward.

When peace, like a river,
Attendeth my way.
When sorrows like sea billows roll;
Whatever my lot, thou hast
taught me to say,
It is well,
It is well with my soul.
It is well with my soul,
It is well,
It is well with my soul.
—Horatio G. Spafford

CONSOLATION
in Times of Loss

For as the sufferings of Christ abound in us, so our consolation also aboundeth by Christ.

—2 Corinthians 1:5

Our loss touches God's heart deeply. He created the one for whom we grieve, and he knows very well the irreplaceable nature of the relationship we shared. God does not minimize or misunderstand our pain. He weeps with us and longs to console us with his love.

Of the many ways to suffer, I feel all of them in this firestorm of sadness. It robs my sleep, saps my strength, and changes me so much I hardly recognize myself. Ease my misery, Lord. Clear my mind as though washing streaks from a window. Hold me when I cry, releasing feelings that keep me sick; send others to hold me, too. Remind me that this pain is temporary and can be relieved, just like my worries.

Have mercy upon me, O Lord, for I am in trouble: mine eye is consumed with grief, yea, my soul and my belly.

—Psalm 31:9

God,

My grief feels as if it will never subside. Everything within me melts like wax when I wake up in the morning and realize all over again what has happened. My life is forever changed. Sometimes I wonder if you are there, but I know you have promised always to be with me. Please hold me close.

Amen.

All around, the storms may churn,
The seas may rage, the fires burn.
But deep within you, you will not fear,
You will have peace when centered there.
For even amidst the tempest wild,
God will be there to guide you, Child.

Woe is me for my hurt! my wound is grievous; but I said, Truly this is a grief, and I must bear it.

—Jeremiah 10:19

Lord,

Help me grieve and go on...go on in new ways you will reveal to me, as I make my faltering way as far as I can. Hold me while I name and mourn all I have lost, weeping and wailing like the abandoned child I feel I am. Then, in time and with you to lean on, I can focus on what I have left.

Amen.

So when this corruptible shall have put on incorruption, and this mortal shall have put on immortality, then shall be brought to pass the saying that is written, Death is swallowed up in victory.

—1 Corinthians 15:54

The passing of a dear one often leaves us wondering "Why, God, why?" If we knew that death is the beginning of a new mystery, a new adventure to unfold, we would feel joy for those who leave this earth and joy for those yet to leave.

Surely he hath borne our griefs, and carried our sorrows: yet we did esteem him stricken, smitten of God, and afflicted.

—Isaiah 53:4

In the depth of my pain, I cry out to God. In grief and sorrow, in loss and anguish, I cry out to God. When I am overwhelmed and cannot bear another moment, I cry out to God. And he hears my cry. He listens and cares and answers, as he always has throughout all time.

When we lose a spouse, we must take time to go within and reaffirm our connection with God. Once we are able to feel God's presence at work in our lives, we will know that we already have all we need to help us move beyond the grief and begin to live and love again.

And said, Where have ye laid him? They said unto him, Lord, come and see. Jesus wept. Then said the Jews, Behold how he loved him!

—John 11:34–36

Like a toddler who falls more than he stands, I'm pulling myself upright in the aftermath of death. I know you as a companion, God of mending hearts, and feel you steadying me. Thank you for the gift of resilience. Lead me to others who have hurt and gone on; I need to see how it's done.

Blessings often come to us
shaded in disguise.

Miracles work magic veiled
from human eyes.

Knowing healing comes from pain,

That every loss makes way for gain,

Or that the sun shines after rain,

And what goes round comes back again,

Marks the difference between
the ignorant and the wise.

Lord, I believe a rest remains,
To all thy people known;
A rest where pure enjoyment reigns
And thou art loved alone;
A rest where all our soul's desire
Is fixed on things above;
Where fear and sin and grief expire,
Cast out by perfect love.
—Charles Wesley

And whether we be afflicted, it is for your consolation and salvation, which is effectual in the enduring of the same sufferings which we also suffer: or whether we be comforted, it is for your consolation and salvation.

—2 Corinthians 1:6

Lord,

I know that part of life is loss and that without loss we cannot treasure the new blessings that come our way. But I am still hurting, and the pain is deep. Help me see the beautiful silver lining that surrounds the dark clouds now hanging overhead.

Amen.

So they sat down with him upon the ground seven days and seven nights, and none spake a word unto him: for they saw that his grief was very great.

—Job 2:13

I am sorrowful after this great tragedy. It feels like this is more than I can bear. Yet I know just crying with others is one way to share the burden. Thank you for other survivors and thank you for healing tears, Father. May they flow freely and turn quickly into the joy that you promise will come.

Come, ye disconsolate,
Where'er ye languish;
Come, at the shrine of God fervently kneel;
Here bring your wounded hearts;
Here tell your anguish;
Earth has no sorrow that
heaven cannot heal.

—Thomas Moore

And the Lord God formed man of the dust of the ground, and breathed into his nostrils the breath of life; and man became a living soul.

—Genesis 2:7

God,

I am not sure how to go on. I am completely devastated. My possessions and my home are now nothing more than dust. Please remind me that you, Creator, formed humans from dust. Console me with the knowledge that I can create beauty from these ruins.

Amen.

Lord,

Time helps, but it never quite blunts the loneliness that loss brings. Thank you for the peace that is slowly seeping into my pores, allowing me to live with the unlivable; to bear the unbearable. Guide and bless my faltering steps down a new road. Prop me up when I think I can't go it alone; prod me when I tarry too long in lonely self-pity.

Most of all, Kind Healer, thank you for the gifts of memory and dreams. The one comforts, the other beckons, both halves of a healing whole.

Amen.

From the dark night of the soul
Comes the blessing of the dawn.
From the deep wounds of the heart
Comes the gift of love reborn.
From the chaos of confusion
Comes the calm of clarity.
From the anguish of discord
Comes the peace of harmony.
From the grieving of great loss
Comes the happiness of new life.
From the coldness of despair
Comes the warmth of our Father's light.

I never meant to be a failure, O God of covenants and promises. I never meant to break vows solemnly made. But I am and I did. Comfort me as I mourn the truth that I could not be okay and remain in that marriage. Comfort me as I leave behind the familiar—friends, surroundings, assumptions, home, and connections. I also lose all of them in this "settlement." Lead me toward other friends and new landmarks, but let this new life not be created quickly and casually, Lord, as if divorce is no more serious than clipping one's fingernails. Enable me to learn something from this grieving passage so that my mistakes don't get repeated and I roll out of one non-okay marriage into another without missing a beat. Be with me now, Lord, as I leave not only a familiar place, but a familiar me. Grant me wisdom to go forward now, toward a new home and life, solitary but free. Be with me; the way home has never seemed longer.

The voice of thy thunder was in the heaven: the lightnings lightened the world: the earth trembled and shook.

—Psalm 77:18

Tree or person, lightning can topple whatever it hits. Console us with your truth that trouble, trauma, tragedy—like lightning—happen sometimes, random and without malice from you. Should it strike, we'll look for rainbows, assured of your presence as we pick up the pieces.

There are few things in life more heartbreaking than the death of a child. One so recently born, exiting life far too soon for our hearts to handle it. A time to be born, and a time to die. But there's supposed to be lots of time in between—a lifetime, in fact. How do we pick up the pieces and go on when our hearts ache as they never have before?

O Lord, it is so hard to see the hope in certain circumstances. I guess we just need time. Time to grieve. Time to regain our balance. Time to renew our trust and hope for the future. While we are going through this season of healing, please hold us close.

When drooping pleasure turns to grief,
And trembling faith is changed to fear,
The murmuring wind, the quivering leaf,
Shall softly tell us, thou are near!
—Oliver Wendell Holmes, Sr.

For I know that my redeemer liveth, and that he shall stand at the latter day upon the earth: And though after my skin worms destroy this body, yet in my flesh shall I see God.

—Job 19:25–26

Job spoke the words of the above passage when his body was covered with painful boils. After previously losing all his wealth and his status, Job was enduring the deterioration of his health while grieving over the loss of his children. Job had always walked uprightly before God, and all of these evils had befallen him nonetheless. How disheartening! Still, even while Job was immersed in pain and on the brink of death, his faith in God did not waver. By focusing on his Redeemer and the eternal life he knew was ahead for him, Job refused to allow anything to rob him of his relationship with God.

Heavenly Father,

It is difficult to talk about death with my children. When friends or relatives die, my children need to know that death is a natural part of life; that this earthly life is not all there is; that we will all meet again in heaven some day.

Yet the earthly loss is painful. It causes loneliness and sorrow and sometimes fear. These feelings can't be readily erased. My children need to know that you are with them.

Help me to find the words that will point them to you, Lord—words that will glorify you, words that will soothe and take away my children's fears. Help me to deal with the sad feelings in tangible ways, so the sorrow is alleviated little by little. Make your presence known to each of my children in their times of need, and shelter them from the sting of death.

Amen.

Sweet hour of prayer, sweet hour of prayer,
That calls me from a world of care
And bids me at my Father's throne
Make all my wants and wishes known!
In seasons of distress and grief,
My soul has often found relief,
And oft escaped the tempter's snare
By thy return, sweet hour of prayer.
—William Walford

For if these things be in you, and abound, they make you that ye shall neither be barren nor unfruitful in the knowledge of our Lord Jesus Christ.

—2 Peter 1:8

Fall is a time of change. Sometimes that change is beautiful, as when the leaves begin to change color. Sometimes that change brings loss, as the days grow shorter and the trees grow bare. Let me never be afraid to change and grow myself—and let me remember that you are with me even in times of loss and sorrow.

Lord,

I ask your blessings today on those who may feel alone and lonely: the ill, the housebound, those in nursing homes, the newly divorced. I ask that they feel a sense of your consoling presence. I ask that those who interact with them be moved with a spirit of kindness. Please instill in me that same spirit of kindness, that I will recognize loneliness and be willing to walk with those who are experiencing it!

Amen.

Strength and honour are her clothing; and she shall rejoice in time to come.

—Proverbs 31:25

Some chapters in life are more difficult than others. My mother, who has been a confidante, a support, and a role model my entire life, was recently diagnosed with dementia. Dementia is a long goodbye, and even as I grieve this loss and help her navigate a very scary new chapter, I am determined to remain present for my husband and our two children. Some days, I struggle against feeling ground down and bitter. Many days, I am angry that this disease is robbing me of my wise mother, and my children of the grandmother they have known. God, I am afraid. Please help me to remain steadfast and honorable in my actions, no matter what turns life takes in the days ahead.

Gently, Lord
Love me gently.
I'm hurting now.
I've lived to see your sovereignty.
You've taught my knees to bow.
I've caught glimpses of your glory.
I've seen your righteous ways.
But right now I need you, Father,
Just to face another day.

And when the Lord saw her, he had compassion on her, and said unto her, Weep not. And he came and touched the bier: and they that bare him stood still. And he said, Young man, I say unto thee, Arise.

—Luke 7:13–14

The widow whose only son died didn't even need to ask Jesus for help. When he saw her desperate grief, he reached out to perform a miracle. I can only imagine her incredulous joy, and how startled and amazed all the mourners must have been.

Those who were bearing the bier must have seen something in this stranger who came to them, that they halted when Jesus came close. May I be attuned to your presence, Jesus, that I stop to allow you to work. I thank you, Jesus, for the unexpected gifts you have given me.

O Lord My God,

Be not thou far from me; my God, have regard to help me; for there have risen up against me sundry thoughts, and great fears, afflicting my soul. How shall I pass through unhurt? How shall I break them to pieces? This is my hope, my one only consolation, to flee unto thee in every tribulation, to trust in thee, to call upon thee from my inmost heart, and to wait patiently for thy consolation

Amen.

—Thomas à Kempis

And our hope of you is stedfast, knowing, that as ye are partakers of the sufferings, so shall ye be also of the consolation.

—2 Corinthians 1:7

Why me, Lord? I have asked that question a million times, when I become ill, or one of my children is hurt. Why me, Lord? And his answer? Why not you? I learned the Lord doesn't pick and choose who suffers. We all suffer at some point in life, and no one is immune. But I also learned whatever suffering the Lord asks me to experience comes with the courage, strength, and compassion to get through it. It's a promise the Lord made to me, that he would never give me more than I could handle. So when things come into my life I'd rather not deal with, I have hope and faith that I can deal with them, with the Lord to guide me.

Our light affliction, which is but for a moment, worketh for us a far more exceeding and eternal weight of glory; while we look not at the things which are seen, but at the things which are not seen: for the things which are seen are temporal; but the things which are not seen are eternal.

—2 Corinthians 4:17–18

Whatever trouble this day or year has held, it has only been momentary. God has been working in you something eternal and unseen, a brightness and splendor beyond your comprehension. It is the full weight of his glory. Don't dwell on the details of previous failures or losses. Instead trust God's work; he is preparing you for an eternity with him.

And Joshua said unto them, Fear not, nor be dismayed, be strong and of good courage: for thus shall the Lord do to all your enemies against whom ye fight.

—Joshua 10:25

God,

Teach me to not fear adversity. It is a mother's kneejerk reaction to protect her children from all trials, but one cannot travel through life without reversals of fortune. Help me to accept and face challenges not only to myself but to my children. My kids will face unkindness; they will face unfairness, loss, and even cruelty in their life's journey. God, help me to remember that adversity breeds character—that we cannot necessarily control what happens to us but we can control our response to it. Grant me the strength to respond to adversity with grace, and please guide me as I give my children the tools to greet life's vicissitudes with faith in you, and with courage.

Amen.

COMFORT
in Times of Distress

Thou shalt increase my greatness,
and comfort me on every side.

—Psalm 71:21

God's grace is our comfort in times of trouble and our beacon of hope amid the blackness of despair. By opening ourselves to God's ever-present grace, we know we are loved and cared for, and our hearts sing out in joyful gratitude.

And Ephraim their father mourned many days, and his brethren came to comfort him.

—1 Chronicles 7:22

God promises us his comfort, but he also uses us as his agents to comfort others. In fact, the difficulties we've gone through often give us the ability to reassure others who are now going through the same experiences. How will God use you to extend comfort to someone else?

Then came there unto him all his brethren, and all his sisters, and all they that had been of his acquaintance before, and did eat bread with him in his house: and they bemoaned him, and comforted him.

—Job 42:11

God does not comfort us to make us comfortable, but to make us comforters.

—John Henry Jowett

Dear Lord,

Each night the news is full of trouble. So much pain and sorrow. It makes me ache to see it all. Some nights, it seems that's all there is; this world seems sometimes so weary and heavy laden. Then I turn to you and know that you are nearest on the darkest days. There is comfort in knowing you and that you have not forsaken us or the people whose world is presently dark.

Amen.

The Lord shall fight for you, and ye shall hold your peace.

—Exodus 14:14

When violence strikes us like mud splashed from a puddle, we bolt our doors and cover our heads. God can draw us from hiding and nudge us to get busy. For violence, like water in a puddle, can only thrive in a hole. Inspired, we can fill it up with hands that, instead of wringing helplessly, are busy rebuilding.

In my distress I called upon the Lord, and cried to my God: and he did hear my voice out of his temple, and my cry did enter into his ears.

—2 Samuel 22:7

Disaster can strike at any time without warning to anyone anywhere. Our lives can change dramatically in one unexpected moment, but in the worst times of our lives, we can lean on family, friends, and even strangers who reach out to us. Yet, even more importantly, we can turn to God, who is always there for us during our darkest hours. He will never fail us, never let us down, and never turn away from us when we cry out to him.

Thou art my hiding place and my shield: I hope in thy word.

—Psalm 119:114

After the storm, they cautiously push open their closet door and creep from their hiding place. How bad is it? They see destruction everywhere. Nothing left untouched, except for one safe spot—the closet in which the whole family crouched, pressed tight together, frightened, holding one another, praying. One thing remains, upright and safe—their hiding place in time of trouble, their sanctuary, the right place to be.

When a long-term relationship comes to an end, it's natural to mourn the loss of a companion and to grieve the death of a particular way of life. But we can mourn and grieve only for so long, then we must ask God to give us the grace and the courage to finally close that door and walk toward a new door waiting to be opened. We must take the next step God has for us.

When the loss of someone we dearly love brings a cold darkness to our lives, it seems that darkness will be forever with us and our hearts will never feel joy again. We believe then that night will never end and day will never come. Yet the darkness will leave and the night will end when we hold on to our Lord, for he will bring light back into our lives. In that light, our hopes will be renewed and a joy will reside in our hearts once again.

To every thing there is a season, and a time to every purpose under the heaven.

—Ecclesiastes 3:1

This is our darkest hour when we feel we cannot suffer any worse. Yet, something inside whispers to us, "To every thing there is a season," and we notice the faint glimmer of hope at the end of this long, dark tunnel of despair. The more we focus on the voice, the louder it becomes. The more we seek the light, the brighter it becomes. This is God's love and compassion for us making itself known, and in his growing presence, we become stronger and our faith is renewed.

This is my comfort in my affliction: for thy word hath quickened me.

—Psalm 119:50

The pain of losing someone dear to us or watching a relationship come to an end can be overwhelming. We feel bereft and alone, confused and lost, certain that we will hurt like this forever. But with God's strength, we can move on.

O spread the tidings 'round,
wherever man is found,

Wherever human hearts and
human woes abound;

Let every Christian tongue
proclaim the joyful sound:

The Comforter has come!

The Comforter has come, the
Comforter has come!

The Holy Ghost from heaven,

The Father's promise given;

O spread the tidings 'round,
wherever man is found—

The Comforter has come!

The long, long night is past, the
morning breaks at last,

And hushed the dreadful wail
and fury of the blast,

As over the golden hills the
day advances fast!

The Comforter has come!

—Francis Bottome

Heavenly Father,

I ask for your healing presence. Protect me from the worldly hurts and evil that have clouded my life and robbed me of joy. Help me forget the past, to let go of grudges, and to make a new start. Take away the darkness of my sorrow, and flood it with the light of your love. Forgive me, so I might forgive others.

Amen.

My Creator,

I know in my heart that these tears will one day give way again to joy, yet for now I know only pain. Help me to find the courage to let these tears flow, to feel the loss and heartbreak, so that I may come out whole and cleansed again. For on the other side of my sorrow I know life waits for me. I want to laugh again.

Amen.

O Joy that seekest me through pain,
I cannot close my heart to thee;
I trace the rainbow through the rain,
And feel the promise is not vain
That morn shall tearless be.

—George Matheson

As the hart panteth after the water brooks, so panteth my soul after thee, O God. My soul thirsteth for God, for the living God: when shall I come and appear before God? My tears have been my meat day and night, while they continually say unto me, Where is thy God?

—Psalm 42:1–3

Comfort us, God, when we come to this awesome conclusion: What did not satisfy us when we finally laid hold of it was surely not the thing we were so long in seeking. Yes, comfort us by this recognition: In all our longings, we are only yearning for you.

Thou tellest my wanderings: put thou my tears into thy bottle: are they not in thy book?

—Psalm 56:8

Thank you, Lord, for reddened eyes. Believing your promise that comfort follows mourning, we bawl and sob. In your wisdom, onion-peeling salty tears differ from cleansing grieving ones; we're grateful for their healing. Deliver us from stiff upper lips, and if we've lost our tears, help us find them.

Lord,

When I'm waiting through the turmoil of doing the right thing at the cost of my personal comfort, help me to be patient. Help me not to sabotage your works by trying to fix things in my own way. Oh, it's not always easy to hold my tongue, but if I wait until you open the door for me to speak—and I look to you for the right attitude when I do talk—then I won't have to deal with all the regrets and what-ifs. Grant me a patient spirit, Father.

Amen.

Lord,

Sometimes I feel like throwing in the towel. I have so many responsibilities, and it is hard to keep up. Some days I juggle everything flawlessly, but then one of those days comes along. I oversleep, and I rush to drop the kids off at school. I arrive at work late, only to realize we have a meeting with an important client, and I am woefully unprepared. I finally get home after working late, and I am met with the news that one of my children is in trouble at school. I feel like a failure on days like this, Lord. Comfort me and fill me with the hope that only you can give. Give me the strength to keep going even when it's hard, so I can revel in the growth that results.

In your name I pray.

And the publican, standing afar off, would not lift up so much as his eyes unto heaven, but smote upon his breast, saying, God be merciful to me a sinner. I tell you, this man went down to his house justified rather than the other: for every one that exalteth himself shall be abased; and he that humbleth himself shall be exalted.

—Luke 18:13–14

On my worst days, I find it comforting to call this parable to mind. On such days I really relate to the tax collector. I feel lost in this world, far from you. Please help me, Lord. Forgive my recent failings and give me the courage, strength, and wisdom to make things right again.

Lord,

You are the God who has set the foundations of the earth, who blessed Abraham with offspring "as numerous as the stars in heaven." You have blessed me, too, by giving me the treasure of my heart, my family. I pour out my thanks for these gifts, which are far above any riches the world can give. How can I praise you enough?

Heavenly Father, I never fail to come to you for help and comfort in the dark times of my life, yet I don't always remember you when my cup is overflowing. Forgive me if I seem ungrateful and take your generosity for granted. How can I forget all that you give me each day?

You bring beauty, peace, and love to my existence. My heart overflows with thanksgiving.

Amen.

For God hath caused me to be fruitful in the land of my affliction.

—Genesis 41:52

Like aching bones that find relief in a steamy, hot bath, O God, that's the comfort I long for. Take from my life the fear, the hurt, the doubt, the unknown, the insecurity—the afflictions. Nonetheless, your promise is to comfort us in our afflictions not remove them. Help me to know that I will experience the "relief" I want only when I am open to accepting your healing comfort that gives us the strength to triumph.

Father God,

Disappointments come to us all, but it is particularly poignant when my children face disappointments. I ache for them; yet there is seldom anything I can do except comfort them.

You give comfort, too, Lord. Your love has been my shield against the world's harsh realities. When I am not able to comfort my children and protect them from disappointment, help them find their comfort in you. And may we all learn to pass along to others that same comfort you have given us.

Amen.

Lord Jesus Christ, in thee alone,
My only hope on earth I place,
For other comforter is none,
No help have I but in thy grace.
There is no man nor creature here,
No angel in the heav'nly sphere,
Who at my call can succor me.
I cry to thee,
In thee I trust implicitly.

—Johannes Schneesing, trans.
Catherine Winkworth

My brethren, count it all joy when ye fall into divers temptations; Knowing this, that the trying of your faith worketh patience.

—James 1:2–3

Lord, motherhood is full of trials that have tested my faith. And, yes, I have developed perseverance and maturity. But like James, I still "count it all joy." In the midst of these trials, I am often ready to give up, to weep and wail over my misfortune; but you are there, Lord, to comfort me. You come to me with your healing touch to wipe away my sorrow.

With your help, Father, I have so far managed to survive each trial intact, with the joy far outweighing the pain. As I hug each of my children and hold them tight, I thank you, Lord.

The past, O God of yesterdays, todays, and promise-filled tomorrows, can be an anchor or a launching pad. It's sometimes so easy to look back on the pain and hurt and believe the future may be an instant replay. Help us to accept the aches of the past and put them in perspective so we can also see the many ways you supported and nurtured us. Then, believing in your promise of regeneration, launch us into the future free and excited to live in joy.

O Lord Jesus Christ,

Thou, good Shepherd of the sheep, who camest to seek the lost, and to gather them to thy fold, have compassion upon those who have wandered from thee; feed those who hunger, cause the weary to lie down in thy pastures, bind up those who are broken in heart, and strengthen those who are weak, that we, relying on thy care and being comforted by thy love, may abide in thy guidance to our lives' end; for thy name's sake.

Amen.

—6th-century prayer

A friend loveth at all times, and a brother is born for adversity.

—Proverbs 17:17

Lord, it hurts to see those we love with tears in their eyes. We want so desperately to take away their pain and comfort them. But as we go to their sides in their time of need, we should not go alone. Only you can offer true comfort. Please add your comfort to ours as we support our friends through these trying times.

Lord,

Lately I really do feel like a tree that has been chopped down. Everything that I've held dear has been taken from me; I feel numb, and my life seems meaningless. Hope seems far away.

I have not forgotten, though, that you are a God of new life. I trust that the sun will shine again and the rain will fall when necessary. It is hard to let go of what was, but I believe that I will grow strong and my heart will again leap for joy rather than merely throb with this dull ache.

My roots are secure in you, Lord—I will not allow myself to remain so shaken. Though the storms of this life uproot and tear down, I will hold steadfast to hope.

Amen.

Lord,

This really hurts. My heart is broken and my faith in love has been shattered. Help me find my way back to wholeness within. I know that one day I will love again, but right now, I am so angry and lost. I know that learning to forgive the one who hurt me is the fastest path to new love, but right now I need all the help I can get just to keep my chin up and my head held high. Help me heal my heart and find it even stronger than before. Help me to one day get to the point where I can forgive, find the lesson in all of this, and move on. Help me show compassion to myself and to the one who caused me this pain.

Help me, Lord.

Blessed are they that mourn:
for they shall be comforted.

—Matthew 5:4

When I drift away from you, it is often sorrow and need that draw me back. In times of crisis, I instinctively turn towards you. Thank you for sending your Spirit of consolation. Let me always remember that gratitude.

Other refuge have I none;
Hangs my helpless soul on thee:
Leave, ah! leave me not alone,
Still support and comfort me.
All my trust on thee is stayed,
All my help from thee I bring;
Cover my defenseless head
With the shadow of thy wing!
—Traditional prayer

Yea, though I walk through the valley of the shadow of death, I will fear no evil: for thou art with me; thy rod and thy staff they comfort me.

—Psalm 23:4

This much-loved psalm reminds us that death is merely a "shadow." The great shepherd will be with us, comforting us, then as always. But death itself is not real for the children of God. "I shall not die, but live, and declare the works of the Lord," David writes elsewhere (Psalm 118:17).

Thus Apostle Paul referred to his own death as "the time of my departure" (2 Timothy 4:6) and elsewhere as "sleep" (1 Corinthians 15:51). When his friend Lazarus died, Jesus told his disciples, "I go, that I may awake him out of sleep." (John 11:11). Believers have no reason to fear death. It is only a shadow. And he is with us.

HEALING
in Times of Sickness

The Lord will strengthen him upon the bed of languishing: thou wilt make all his bed in his sickness.

—Psalm 41:3

When illness strikes, the effects go beyond the physical suffering. Fear, despair, and terrible isolation arise as the illness prolongs itself. It feels natural to lash out at your failing body, medicine that does not help, and even at the God who allowed this terrible thing to happen to you. The fate of the patient's loved ones can be equally painful, as they stand by feeling helpless to be of any real assistance. Yet, be assured that the Lord is there among you.

Holy Spirit, the life that gives life.

You are the cause of all movement;

You are the breath of all creatures;

You are the salve that purifies our souls;

You are the ointment that
heals our wounds;

You are the fire that warms our hearts;

You are the light that guides our feet.

Let all the world praise you.

—Hildegard of Bingen

When Jesus heard that, he said, This sickness is not unto death, but for the glory of God, that the Son of God might be glorified thereby.

—John 11:4

Is illness your will, Lord? I need answers, for I want you to help me heal. But if you send illness, how can I trust you to heal? Reassure me that you will work everything out eventually. And when that isn't possible, be with me as I suffer. Freed from fear I can get stronger as your healing energy flows through me, restoring me to my abundant life.

It is like a grain of mustard seed, which, when it is sown in the earth, is less than all the seeds that be in the earth: But when it is sown, it groweth up, and becometh greater than all herbs, and shooteth out great branches; so that the fowls of the air may lodge under the shadow of it.

—Mark 4:31–32

O God,

Healing is going so-o-o-o slowly, and I am impatient and grumpy. Mind, body, or soul, this could take a long time. Remind me that recovery is a journey, not a hasty jet-lagged arrival. Bless me with faith to sustain me, step by small step. You do miraculous things with faith as tiny as mustard seeds that, in time, blossom into awesome growth. I hold that picture as I make mustard-seed progress along the road to healing.

Amen.

The good Teacher, the Wisdom, the Word of the Father, who created us, cares for the entire nature of his creation. This all-sufficient Physician of humanity, the Savior, heals both body and soul.

—Clement of Alexandria

But they that wait upon the Lord shall renew their strength; they shall mount up with wings as eagles; they shall run, and not be weary; and they shall walk, and not faint.

—Isaiah 40:31

Great Physician,

Help me recover from this ambush of illness and the worry it brings. Reassure my fearful heart that my sickness was never intended; it just happened. Bodies break down, parts age, and minds weary. Your assurance gives me strength to hang on.

Amen.

Offer the sacrifices of righteousness, and put your trust in the Lord.

—Psalm 4:5

Sitting here in this waiting room, O God, time drags and fear festers. Remake worry into energized, active prayers, into trust in the process of healing and recovery. We're scooting over to make room for you, a companion for the waiting.

There is a balm in Gilead
To make the wounded whole;
There is a balm in Gilead
To heal the sin-sick soul.
Some times I feel discouraged,
And think my work's in vain,
But then the Holy Spirit
Revives my soul again.
If you can't preach like Peter,
If you can't pray like Paul,
Just tell the love of Jesus,
And say he died for all.
There is a balm in Gilead
To make the wounded whole;
There is a balm in Gilead
To heal the sin-sick soul.
—African American spiritual

And when he heard that it was Jesus of Nazareth, he began to cry out, and say, Jesus, thou son of David, have mercy on me.

—Mark 10:47

Dear God, the pain is so great and unbearable that I feel as though another moment of it will tear me apart. Please rescue me from this pain. Touch my body and heal me. Hear my pleas, for only you have the power to deliver me from my affliction. Have mercy upon me. I cry out to you day and night, and I will turn to no one but you.

Then went he down, and dipped himself seven times in Jordan, according to the saying of the man of God: and his flesh came again like unto the flesh of a little child, and he was clean.

—2 Kings 5:14

The outlook is promising, progress steady. Yet, O God, we're afraid to relax for fear illness will sneak up again. Guide us through these shaky days of recovery. Remind us that if we've done it once, we can outwit illness if it dares strike again. As veterans of this illness, we have the scars to prove it!

O God,

Illness requires new math, subtraction
of old fears and addition of new thought.
Help me bring this lesson home as I draw
ten stick figures, color the percentage
said to recover from this ailment, and
write my name on the brightest figure!
A most deserving child, I praise you
for the resources to make it happen.
Sharing with you divides my troubles
and multiplies my healing chances.

Amen.

When the even was come, they brought unto him many that were possessed with devils: and he cast out the spirits with his word, and healed all that were sick: That it might be fulfilled which was spoken by Esaias the prophet, saying, Himself took our infirmities, and bare our sicknesses.

—Matthew 8:16–17

Thank you, Lord, for enduring unimaginable pain, even to the point of death, so that my broken relationship with my heavenly Father can be healed. By that healing, may all my emotional wounds be healed as well. In your name, I pray.

O Lord my God, I cried unto thee, and thou hast healed me. O Lord, thou hast brought up my soul from the grave: thou hast kept me alive, that I should not go down to the pit.

—Psalm 30:2–3

Dear God,

I come to you today humbled and grateful for the powerful healing you have given me. I was so ill and broken, and weak in body and spirit, and I was losing my faith that I would ever feel good again. Yet you took care of me. Your love provided me with all the medicine I could ever need, and the hope of your eternal presence motivated me to stay in faith, even when things seemed so bleak. I thank you from the bottom of my heart for this new sense of well-being and health, and for knowing that if I stay positive and hopeful, your loving will for me will prevail over any disease or challenge.

Amen.

Heal us, Emmanuel, hear our prayer; we wait to feel thy touch; deep-wounded souls to thee repair, and Savior, we are such.

—William Cowper

I have shewed you all things, how that so labouring ye ought to support the weak, and to remember the words of the Lord Jesus, how he said, It is more blessed to give than to receive.

—Acts 20:35

Someone I care about is suffering, Lord, and I feel helpless. Assure me that a little means a lot and that I'm sharing your healing love in my notes and visits. If you need me to do more, send me. I am like dandelion fluff, small but mighty in possibility.

As an eagle stirreth up her nest, fluttereth over her young, spreadeth abroad her wings, taketh them, beareth them on her wings: So the Lord alone did lead him.

—Deuteronomy 32:11–12

God,

I pray to you today for the healing that only you can bring. I long to be free from pain and suffering, to be whole again in body, mind, and spirit. Give to me the soothing balm of your tender, loving care that I might mount up on wings of eagles and fly with ease again.

Amen.

Lord,

Mothers always worry about their children's health yet often neglect their own. I plead guilty. Too much anxiety, too little sleep, and too little time for trips to the doctor all take their toll on my body and leave me open to illness.

I owe it to my family, Lord, to stay healthy. They depend on me for so many things that my illness would put a strain on them. Please help me to be sensible: to get enough rest, cut down on stress, and seek medical help when needed.

Most of all, I need your healing Spirit to touch me as I come to you in prayer, so I may continue to honor you through service to my family.

Amen.

Lord,

The only blessing I ask for these days is to restore my body to good health. When I am healthy and strong, everything else seems easier and I have the fortitude to handle challenges that come my way. Bless me with good health and vitality, and help me treat my body right and avoid stress when I can.

Amen.

When I don't feel well, it is easy to feel sorry for myself. Then I remember the people who support me and help me when I am unwell. Thank you for the friends and family, the neighbors and coworkers, the nurses and doctors, and everyone else who goes out of the way to brighten my day and make me see a ray of light in the darkness.

And there came a leper to him, beseeching him, and kneeling down to him, and saying unto him, If thou wilt, thou canst make me clean. And Jesus, moved with compassion, put forth his hand, and touched him, and saith unto him, I will; be thou clean.

—Mark 1:40–41

There is no problem too big for God to help us with it, no wound or hurt too deep for healing. Cleanse us, Lord, of all that hurts us and hinders us emotionally, spiritually, and physically.

O God,

Who by the grace of the Holy Ghost hast poured the gifts of love into the hearts of thy faithful people, grant unto all thy servants in thy mercy health of body and soul, that they may love thee with all their strength, and with perfect affection fulfill thy pleasure; through Jesus Christ our Lord.

Amen.

—6th-century prayer

O Holy Creator,

Who hath bound together heaven and earth, let me walk through your kingdom comforted and protected by the warm rays of your love. Let me be healed as I stand basking in the divine light of your presence, where strength and hope and joy are found. Let me sit at rest in the valley of your peace, surrounded by the fortress of your loving care.

Amen.

Take this burden from me, Lord,
Free me from this pain.
Let me move with ease and grace
And walk in health again.
Take this yoke upon you, Lord,
And help me toward my goal,
I'm tired of being sick and tired
And long to be made whole.
Release me from my illness
And restore me to my best.
If you can do that for me, Lord,
I'll take care of the rest.

The Lord is my light and my salvation; whom shall I fear? the Lord is the strength of my life; of whom shall I be afraid?

—Psalm 27:1

In the midst of the darkness that threatens to overwhelm us lies a pinpoint of light, a persistent flicker that guides us through the pain and fear, through the hopelessness and despair, to a place of peace and healing on the other side. This is God's Spirit, leading us back home like the lighthouse beacon that directs the ships through the fog to the safety of the harbor.

And Jesus went about all Galilee, teaching in their synagogues, and preaching the gospel of the kingdom, and healing all manner of sickness and all manner of disease among the people.

—Matthew 4:23

Lord,

You do not leave us to suffer alone. You are with us in pain, in sickness, and in our worst moments. Thank you for your comfort and healing power. Thank you for getting us through when our bodies fail, when our health falters, and when we need you most of all.

Amen.

Dearest God,

My body is slowing, and I am in need of healing. I am scared of illness and of what lies ahead. I ask now for your healing light to shine upon me and favor me with your grace. I ask now for your love. I give myself to you, God, and I pray that you will help me and heal me.

Amen.

When thou passest through the waters, I will be with thee; and through the rivers, they shall not overflow thee: when thou walkest through the fire, thou shalt not be burned; neither shall the flame kindle upon thee.

—Isaiah 43:2

The final healing, O God, is near, and my body is painfully ready. Help me think of this as a "birthing pain," for I'm in the process of becoming new. Deliver me onto that other shore newly born and healed from this life's travail. Hold my hand, for pain's waves are building into a sea strong enough for us to walk across at last.

GUIDANCE
in Times of Confusion

But ye, beloved, building up yourselves on your most holy faith, praying in the Holy Ghost, Keep yourselves in the love of God, looking for the mercy of our Lord Jesus Christ unto eternal life.

—Jude 1:20–21

Each prayer is a message of faith in God. We are saying, "I trust you; lead me. I believe in you; guide me. I need you; show me." When we offer ourselves openly, he will always answer.

To open their eyes, and to turn them from darkness to light, and from the power of Satan unto God, that they may receive forgiveness of sins, and inheritance among them which are sanctified by faith that is in me.

—Acts 26:18

Like the lighthouse beacon, faith guides our way through the fog of fear, doubt, and uncertainty to the sea of clarity beyond.

Lord, you are here,
Lord, you are there.
You are wherever we go.
Lord, you guide us,
Lord, you protect us.
You are wherever we go.
Lord, we need you,
Lord, we trust you,
You are wherever we go.
Lord, we love you,
Lord, we praise you,
You are wherever we go.

And he said, Come. And when Peter was come down out of the ship, he walked on the water, to go to Jesus. But when he saw the wind boisterous, he was afraid; and beginning to sink, he cried, saying, Lord, save me.

—Matthew 14:29–30

Sometimes I'm like Peter, and I walk on water. I stand above my circumstances, which are like the swirling tempests of the sea. But then, like Peter, I take my eyes off Jesus and concentrate on things below. Soon I start to sink. How I long to have a consistent, water-walking, eyes-on-Jesus faith.

And therefore will the Lord wait, that he may be gracious unto you, and therefore will he be exalted, that he may have mercy upon you: for the Lord is a God of judgment: blessed are all they that wait for him.

—Isaiah 30:18

Throughout life, one of the hardest words to hear is WAIT. Sometimes we may anxiously wonder, "Where is God when I need him?" And yet we are reminded in Scripture that patience is developed through faithful waiting. God has a design in even the most difficult situations that will enable our character to become stronger. As we learn patience, we also learn to trust that God has our best interests in mind. He cannot abandon us, and he will always rescue us at just the right time.

Get wisdom, get understanding: forget it not; neither decline from the words of my mouth.

—Proverbs 4:5

The Bible urges us to seek wisdom and understanding. We are instructed to have two goals: Wisdom—knowing and doing right—and common sense. Wisdom is the ability to meet each situation with discernment and good judgment, whether in dealing with others, making choices, or dispensing justice. Wisdom involves using the knowledge we have to take the proper course of action—if we know and don't act, it is the same as not knowing at all. When we let Christ become the source of our wisdom, he will guide us in making wise decisions and acting on them.

Pray without ceasing,
Let your love illumine the skies
That the darkness of man may drop away
And only the light of God show through.
Pray unto the Holy,
With all your heart and soul.
Pray for the shining light of guidance
That your path may be glorious with love.
—St. Augustine

And he said unto him, If now I have found grace in thy sight, then shew me a sign that thou talkest with me.

—Judges 6:17

How lonely we are when trouble strikes. Send us a sign, Lord. We long for a message, a hand reaching toward us. And just as God promised, we're visited by a Presence in dream and daylight revelations, and we are grateful for God's personal, one-on-one caring.

It seems so insignificant,
This choice you have to make.
Yet the Lord can use small acts of faith
To cause the earth to shake!
So pray and wait to know his will
For decisions made today,
And the Lord may use your faithfulness
To show someone the way.

I said in mine heart, God shall judge the righteous and the wicked: for there is a time there for every purpose and for every work.

—Ecclesiastes 3:17

We can look ahead with hope and behind with satisfaction. We can look ahead with fear and behind with regret. But we must never do either so much that we miss today.

Blessed be the God of Shadrach, Meshach, and Abednego, who hath sent his angel, and delivered his servants that trusted in him, and have changed the king's word, and yielded their bodies, that they might not serve nor worship any god, except their own God.

—Daniel 3:28

Thousands of angels at God's command comfort, encourage, and guide us through the trials of our daily existence.

O may thy spirit guide my feet
In ways of righteousness;
Make every path of duty straight,
And plain before my face.
Amen.
—Joachim Neander

Lord,

Somebody hates me and is trying to get others to hate me, too. How quickly bad news travels. Okay, I think, I'll just hate back. I don't want to pray for this hateful person, even as I admit life must be rough to make them so mean-spirited. Hey, but does that make hating okay? Help me balance compassion for haters with accountability. This prayer has no end, for I need to work through this. Help me and soon, for there are real wounds in your world to heal, not just my hurt feelings.

Amen.

Dear God,

As I rise each day, give me the strength, courage, and patience to do the best I can for my family. All through the day, guide me with your grace and divine direction into right action and right decision. And when the day is done and it is time for me to rest my weary mind and body, take the burden of my troubles from me so that I can sleep. Watch over me and mine throughout the night, and when it is time to arise to a new day, be there for me all over again.

Amen.

Lord,

It nearly drives me to distraction to hear my children arguing over trifles. Each wants what the other has. When one says something, the other contradicts. I try, but there seems to be no way to avoid these battles.

I need your steadying hand, Father, to help me cope. Only you can calm the waters of discontent that swirl around them and plant peace within their hearts.

Soothe us with the balm of your Holy Spirit so my children can live together in pleasant harmony.

Amen.

Hold up my goings in thy paths, that my footsteps slip not.

—Psalm 17:5

I can look over my shoulder and see times when you, Pathfinding God, were a ready and dependable companion. I couldn't have done it without you. And I believe that you are already waiting to take my hand into tomorrow—knowledge that gives me the security to risk.

O God, from whom to be turned is to fall,
To whom to be turned is to rise,
And with whom to stand
is to abide for ever;
Grant us in all our duties your help,
In all our perplexities your guidance,
In all our dangers your protection,
And in all our sorrows your peace,
Through Jesus Christ our Lord.
—St. Augustine

Howbeit when he, the Spirit of truth, is come, he will guide you into all truth: for he shall not speak of himself; but whatsoever he shall hear, that shall he speak: and he will shew you things to come.

—John 16:13

Even if my motives are pure, O God, I need to step back and let you guide—all of us—instead of trying to control. Often my mouth is open before I think. Keep me quiet for the sake of peace and learning.

In all things, give thanks.

In the good days of laughter
and joy, give thanks.

In the bad days of struggle
and strife, give thanks.

In the brightest moments and the
darkest hours, give thanks.

In the flow of blessings
and the apparent lack of
goodness, give thanks.

In the face of fortune and
misfortune, give thanks.

In the presence of pleasure
and pain, give thanks.

In all things, give thanks.

For lessons and blessings are
found not just in the light,
but in the darkness.

Over and over I ask myself, "What can I do?" What can I do to make a difference? One of the hardest things about reaching out is having others think I can "fix it" and then finding out that I can't. Lord, help me to remember that what you promise is not to "fix it" for us but rather to give us whatever it takes to prevail in spite of our hurts. Help me keep in mind that sometimes all that is necessary is a listening ear.

I know that releasing control to you, Lord, is one of the hardest but most rewarding steps of obedience that I will ever take. Trusting in your faithfulness and submitting to your authority may seem like leaping headfirst into a river; I feel safe standing on the shoreline, looking at the roaring rapids below, but I know I'm missing out on your best plans for my life. Yes, jumping into the river will sweep me away to places unknown—and it will take all of my strength and effort to navigate the waters—but the adventure will be so worth it!

I want to trust in your faithfulness. I believe that you have great things in store for me. You won't lead me down a river only to abandon me or leave me injured on the riverbed. My soul is precious to you, and you have a purpose in mind for my life. You are faithful, and I will claim that truth as I jump headfirst toward my destiny.

The morning bright
With rosy light
Has waked me from my sleep;
Father, I own
Thy love alone
Thy little one doth keep.
All through the day,
I humbly pray,
Be thou my Guard and Guide;
My sins forgive
And let me live,
Blest Jesus, near thy side. Amen.
—Traditional prayer

And wisdom and knowledge shall be the stability of thy times, and strength of salvation: the fear of the Lord is his treasure.

—Isaiah 33:6

Lord,

Make me strong in body and in spirit. Give me a faith that never weakens, and a courage that never wavers. Help me, Lord, to be a rock to those who need me, as you always are to me. Help me to also help myself when no one is around, and to learn to lean on your wisdom and guidance rather than my own. Be my rock and my shield, guarding me from harm.

Amen.

The words of a man's mouth are as deep waters, and the wellspring of wisdom as a flowing brook.

—Proverbs 18:4

When I am wrong, I turn within to find the right way. God's eternal wisdom is like a flowing river I can tap into at any time, especially when I am clueless and don't know which way to turn. I take comfort in knowing I don't have to be a genius and figure out every last detail of my life. God knows best, and as long as I stay in tune with his Word, I will be divinely inspired.

If any of you lack wisdom, let him ask of God, that giveth to all men liberally, and upbraideth not; and it shall be given him.

—James 1:5

What does the wisdom of God sound like? Like a soft whisper from within. What does the wisdom of God look like? Signs and miracles, big and small, that point to the answers to our problems. What does the wisdom of God feel like? Like a soft, comforting blanket on a cold day that wraps around us. It sounds, looks, and feels like love.

For I know the thoughts that I think toward you, saith the Lord, thoughts of peace, and not of evil, to give you an expected end.

—Jeremiah 29:11

What we desire must align with what God wants for us. Dreams fulfilled are dreams chosen by the one who knows us and loves us most. God always directs our plans to the outcome he knows is best.

And when he was come into his own country, he taught them in their synagogue, insomuch that they were astonished, and said, Whence hath this man this wisdom, and these mighty works?

—Matthew 13:54

The wisdom and insight we need is often hidden in plain sight, right before our eyes, and under our very noses. God is always guiding us, if we stop and open our hearts and spirits to the still, small whisperings within that point the way.

Thou shalt guide me with thy counsel, and afterward receive me to glory.

—Psalm 73:24

You must first see in your mind's eye what you wish to achieve. Feel it in your heart. Then align yourself with God's will and go forth to achieve it, following his inner guidance. This is the only true secret to success!

Write thy blessed name, O Lord, upon my heart, there to remain so indelibly engraven, that no prosperity, no adversity shall ever move me from thy love. Be thou to me a strong tower of defence, a comforter in tribulation, a deliverer in distress, a very present help in trouble, and a guide to heaven through the many temptations and dangers of this life. Amen.

—Thomas à Kempis

But Noah found grace in the eyes of the Lord.

—Genesis 6:8

Let me set my compass to your will, Lord. Let me not be afraid to follow you, even if that pits me against the world's values. Give me a humble heart, Lord, so that I will not judge others—but please give me the gift of moral clarity as well, to seek to live by your values and do your will.